BEHOLD YOUR MOTHER

Marian Stations of the Cross

MARGE STEINHAGE FENELON

Our Sunday Visitor
Huntington, Indiana

Nihil Obstat
Msgr. Michael Heintz, Ph.D.
Censor Librorum

Imprimatur
✠ Kevin C. Rhoades
Bishop of Fort Wayne-South Bend
July 22, 2023

The *Nihil Obstat* and *Imprimatur* are official declarations that a book is free from doctrinal or moral error. It is not implied that those who have granted the *Nihil Obstat* and *Imprimatur* agree with the contents, opinions, or statements expressed.

Excerpts from the *Revised Standard Version of the Bible*—Second Catholic Edition (Ignatius Edition) Copyright © 2006 National Council of the Churches of Christ in the United States of America. Used by permission. All rights reserved worldwide.

Every reasonable effort has been made to determine copyright holders of excerpted materials and to secure permissions as needed. If any copyrighted materials have been inadvertently used in this work without proper credit being given in one form or another, please notify Our Sunday Visitor in writing so that future printings of this work may be corrected accordingly.

Copyright © 2023 by Marge Steinhage Fenelon

Original copyright © 2007 Margaret Steinhage Fenelon, published by Icon Press, 816 W. National Avenue, Milwaukee, WI 53204; 414-672-4432.

28 27 26 25 24 23   1 2 3 4 5 6 7 8 9

All rights reserved. With the exception of short excerpts for critical reviews, no part of this work may be reproduced or transmitted in any form or by any means whatsoever without permission from the publisher. For more information, visit: www.osv.com/permissions.

Our Sunday Visitor Publishing Division
Our Sunday Visitor, Inc.
200 Noll Plaza
Huntington, IN 46750
www.osv.com
1-800-348-2440

ISBN: 978-1-63966-151-0 (Inventory No. T2860)
1. RELIGION—Prayerbooks—Christian.
2. RELIGION—Christian Living—Prayer.
3. RELIGION—Christianity—Catholic.

Cover and interior design: Amanda Falk
Cover and interior art: AdobeStock

PRINTED IN THE UNITED STATES OF AMERICA

To Our Lady of Sorrows

When Jesus saw his mother, and the disciple whom he loved standing near, he said to his mother, "Woman, behold, your son!" Then he said to the disciple, "Behold, your mother!" And from that hour the disciple took her to his own home.

— John 19:26–27

Preface

For centuries, Catholics have meditated on the Stations of the Cross, mentally and emotionally walking up the hill of Calvary with Our Lord. Because it's such a popular prayer, there's a plentitude of versions available. What makes this one different?

It's inspired by the writings of Fr. Joseph Kentenich, founder of the Schoenstatt Apostolic Movement, an international movement of Catholic renewal. From his earliest days, Father Kentenich had a deep attachment to the Blessed Virgin Mary and a profound understanding of her unique role in our salvation.

"Only after she had freely said — again, in the name of mankind — the required yes to the death of the Redeemer, only after she had freely renounced her mother-rights in favor of our claim over him, only after she had surrendered him for the sake of our sins and united her sacrifice with his — only then could the Savior exclaim in accordance with the precise unfolding of God's plan, 'It is consummated!' (Jn 19:30)," Father Kentenich wrote in 1954.

This book is written from the perspective of a child who is witnessing the unspeakable anguish of the Mother of the Redeemer due to the atrocious suffering of her only Son. The child knows that he's partially to blame for this torment and wishes somehow to console the grieving mother. Yet she's confidently resigned to God's perfect plan, and so they climb Calvary together.

Allow yourself to become the devoted child who takes this mother as his own and yearns to soothe her grief. You are that child, and she is your mother. As he hung dying on the Cross, our Lord entrusted Mary to the care of Saint John and Saint John to the care of Mary. Looking down lovingly at Mary, he said, "Woman, behold your son!" Then, looking to Saint John, he said, "Behold, your mother!" (cf. Jn 19:26–27). In that moment, Saint John represented all humankind. In one of his last acts on this earth, Jesus entrusted his mother to us, and us to his mother in a loving relationship meant to last forever. *Ecce mater tua* — behold your mother!

Opening Prayer

Father, I want to walk the way of the cross as a child. Take from me all pretentiousness and inhibition so that, as a child, I can be open to the inspirations of the Holy Spirit as I meditate and pray. Through childlike eyes, let me see the suffering of my mother as she accompanies the Savior to Golgotha. Through a childlike mind, let me experience her suffering, so that I may more clearly understand your will. Through a childlike heart, let me feel her suffering, so that I may be intimately drawn into her Immaculate Heart. Through her, let me finally be entirely converted. Amen.

Jesus Is Condemned to Death

V: We adore you, O Christ, and we praise you.
R: Because by your holy Cross, you have redeemed the world.

Leader: I'm scared! Mother, take my hand and let me stay beside you. The crowd is so loud and violent that it shakes me. How can this be? Just a short time ago they were following Jesus everywhere, pleading with him to work another miracle and pressing him to teach them more about his Father's kingdom. Now they've bound him like a criminal and put him before Pontius Pilate. Instead of shouting, "Crucify him!" they should be shouting, "Have mercy on us!"

Surely this means that Jesus will die a horrible death. Yet, no one comes to his defense. Even you, Mother, remain silent. Why?

All: Mother, I'm the guilty one, not Jesus. He's paying for my sins. If only I could learn to be gentle of heart and accept injustice in humility, your Son wouldn't have to suffer. Please, destroy all the pride in my heart and make it as pure as yours.

SECOND STATION
Jesus Accepts His Cross

V: We adore you, O Christ, and we praise you.
R: Because by your holy Cross, you have redeemed the world.

Leader: Jesus' flesh has been so ripped apart by the soldiers' scourges that I can barely see anything left of it. With his head penetrated by the thorns and his body a bloody mass, there can't be much strength left in him. Yet, Jesus accepts the cross as if he were embracing something precious. How will he ever make it up the hill to Golgotha?

Mother, your eyes are full of pain and your muscles are tense — almost as if you're trying to lift the cross for him. It must be hard for you to hold yourself back as they thrust the heavy wood upon your Son's shoulders. But you do hold back so that the evil one can be conquered and my sins forgiven.

All: I want to ease your pain, but how can I? I'm so weak. Pray for me to have the strength to carry the splinter of the cross the heavenly Father sends me through the difficulties in my own life.

THIRD STATION
Jesus Falls the First Time

V: We adore you, O Christ, and we praise you.
R: Because by your holy Cross, you have redeemed the world.

Leader: Already Jesus faltered, and he's only begun to climb Calvary. There's so much confusion. The soldiers are shouting, kicking, and beating Jesus. How is that going to help him get up? Don't they realize who's beneath that cross?

Mother, I heard you gasp as the cross went down. You know the weight is nearly too much for your Son. I know that the cross is so heavy because it represents the sins of mankind. Our failures — my failures — are what made Jesus fall. But his love for us, his love for me, makes him get up and go on.

All: Sometimes the burden of my own sins and failures brings me down. I falter when I depend on my own power and believe that I can do things by myself. That's when I need you most, Mother. Hold on to me and help me up.

Jesus Meets His Mother

V: We adore you, O Christ, and we praise you.
R: Because by your holy Cross, you have redeemed the world.

Leader: It's taken so long for Jesus to reach this spot on the hill. It's difficult to look at him because his torment is so profound. But at the same time, it's impossible to look away because I know that my sins have contributed to his affliction.

There's a break in the crowd. If we hurry, you can get closer to him, speak to him, touch him. As your eyes meet his and you reach out to him, I can see the love that draws you together. I can understand now that you must suffer silently along with him because your hearts are as one in following the heavenly Father's will.

All: Mother, I'm sorry that you must endure this because of me. Is there any way I can make up for your pain? I love you. Please accept me as your child and shelter me in your heart. I want to belong freely and entirely to you.

FIFTH STATION

Simon of Cyrene Helps Jesus Carry the Cross

V: We adore you, O Christ, and we praise you.
R: Because by your holy Cross, you have redeemed the world.

Leader: I can see the guards grabbing a man from along the side of the road. He seems disturbed by the interruption and doesn't want to comply with their orders to help Jesus carry the cross. Doesn't he realize who Jesus is? If he understood, he would help willingly.

You sighed just now, Mother. It must bring you some comfort to know that someone is finally helping your Son. I wish I could help, but I'm too small in my humanness. Soon Simon will know who Jesus is and be happy that he helped him.

All: Mother, if I were Simon, would I have acted differently? Please pray for me to become strong enough to help Jesus by carrying my own cross, and boldly bearing witness to him in all I do and say.

Veronica Wipes the Face of Jesus

V: We adore you, O Christ, and we praise you.
R: Because by your holy Cross, you have redeemed the world.

Leader: Who is that woman pushing through the crowds? She's not paying any attention to the guards' threats. She's so brave! She must understand who Jesus is, and that's why she won't let Satan stop her from going to him.

Even amid your sorrow, the faint shadow of a smile crosses your lips, Mother, and there's a spark of thankfulness in your eyes. I know that in your heart you're returning the love of this courageous young woman. In your mind, you're uttering a prayer of gratitude for the compassion she's showing your Son by wiping his face with her veil.

All: Mother, how many times have I fallen victim to my own insecurities and denied compassion to someone else? Pray for me to be brave enough to overcome the obstacles that hold me back. May Jesus' countenance be forever impressed upon my heart and mind like it was on Veronica's veil.

SEVENTH STATION
Jesus Falls the Second Time

V: We adore you, O Christ, and we praise you.
R: Because by your holy Cross, you have redeemed the world.

Leader: The cross falls even harder this time, hurtling Jesus to the ground beneath it. The thud rises above the crowd and resonates between the buildings. How desperate Satan is to deter the Savior from his mission. The soldiers still don't seem to understand that shouts and beatings will do no good in making Jesus get on his way. I wish I could tell them myself.

Open your eyes, Mother. Look, Jesus is getting up again. Your love pulls him up and sustains him. If you can be strong, he can be strong too. You are united in a holy two-in-oneness for the sake of my redemption.

All: I'm humiliated whenever I fail. What's worse, I often fail many times in the same endeavor. Then I don't even want to dare trying again. Mother, your love must pull me up and sustain me when I fall so that I can fulfill the mission God has given me.

EIGHTH STATION

Jesus Meets the Weeping Women

V: We adore you, O Christ, and we praise you.
R: Because by your holy Cross, you have redeemed the world.

Leader: The sobs of the women are so miserable that it makes me want to cry along with them. They cry at the shocking sight before them, but do they really understand what's happening? They don't see Jesus as the Redeemer of the World; they see him as a pitiable human being. They don't know that this is the only way to break Satan's hold on mankind.

Mother, when you placed your hand to your heart, I realized that you must feel the women's pain just as you feel your Son's pain. How wonderful it would be if you could explain to them that Jesus' suffering will bring us the joy of salvation.

All: Mother, I'm often like those women. I cry when, in human terms, all seems lost. It's easy to thank God when times are great; it's hard to thank him when times are bleak. Mother, help me to see, as you did, that all parts of God's plan for me are signs of his love.

NINTH STATION

Jesus Falls the Third Time

V: We adore you, O Christ, and we praise you.
R: Because by your holy Cross, you have redeemed the world.

Leader: It's almost as if Satan has laughingly taken hold of the cross and cast it down to the ground. Jesus has fallen so hard that I can't imagine he'll be able to get up again. In his human form, he seems too weak to counter the devil's vengeance a third time. But as Son of God, he will be victorious. Nothing can get in the way of his love for us and his determination to secure our salvation.

Hatred for Satan flares in your eyes, Mother, as you watch him battle with Jesus over the cross. Because you're the Savior's helpmate you, too, are determined to secure our salvation through the crucifixion. You await the destruction of the evil one's realm so that I can be happy in heaven for all eternity.

All: Mother, I so often forget the depths of the love your Son has for me. Because of that, I easily fall for Satan's tricks and deceptions. I know that grieves you even more! Please help me to stand firm against the evil one, as you and Jesus did on Good Friday.

Jesus Is Stripped of His Garments

V: We adore you, O Christ, and we praise you.
R: Because by your holy Cross, you have redeemed the world.

Leader: Even though I'm not the one being stripped, I feel ashamed. No one should be humiliated in this way, much less the King of Kings. Chills run down my back and limbs as I look at Jesus. Yet he bears this vulgar insult to his dignity. It amazes me that, despite the offensiveness of the soldiers, Jesus stands nobly as a symbol of purity. He doesn't allow his nakedness to diminish his royalty.

You pull your mantle more closely around you, Mother. Is that your shivering I feel? It's as if you wish to shield the body of your Son by shielding your own body. You both bear this disgrace because I have so often succumbed to the temptations of impurity in thought and action.

All: Mother, wrap your mantle around me so that I can be a royal child of the Father — a noble symbol of purity.

Jesus Is Nailed to the Cross

V: We adore you, O Christ, and we praise you.
R: Because by your holy Cross, you have redeemed the world.

Leader: The strokes of the executioner's hammer pound right through my heart. Jesus must have swung his carpenter's hammer countless times over wood, forcing nails to penetrate and thus create something beautiful. As he worked, did he ever think of the nails that would someday penetrate his own flesh and bind it against the wood of the cross? Blood spurts forth from the hands that have so often built, blessed, and healed. The executioner is Satan's instrument of destruction. He doesn't know that he's really creating something indescribably beautiful — our salvation.

Your hands have turned white because you're pressing your palms together with such force, Mother. You feel the nails, too, don't you? Still, you make no protest.

All: Mother, I can't stand knowing that I'm to blame for this horrible scene. Please forgive me; pray for me. May I never do anything to make the executioner's hammer swing again.

TWELFTH STATION
Jesus Dies on the Cross

V: We adore you, O Christ, and we praise you.
R: Because by your holy Cross, you have redeemed the world.

Leader: The darkness and silence make me uneasy. I can hear Jesus' slow and shallow breathing. I wish I could breathe for him, but that will only prolong his terrible anguish. The ground beneath the cross is soaked with the blood of the Sacrificial Lamb. That blood should be mine, not his. How can he love me this much?

Please stop crying, Mother. Your grief overwhelms me. Your Son is leaving you, but I'm here. I'll stay beside you. I promise.

Listen! Jesus is asking his Father to forgive his murderers. I'm one of them, aren't I, Mother? Sorrow and devotion fill his eyes as he looks at you for the last time. Will you agree to his request to take me as your child and give yourself to me as my mother? How can you love me this much?

All: I want to be yours forever. Mother, accept me as I am right now — a helpless, imperfect child. Through your love, transform me into the child my Father wants me to be.

Jesus Is Placed in the Arms of His Mother

V: We adore you, O Christ, and we praise you.
R: Because by your holy Cross, you have redeemed the world.

Leader: You take Jesus into your arms as gently as you did when he was a baby. The brow you kiss is no longer soft and smooth, but gashed and bloodied by the thorns of the crown. The delicate hands you once tenderly held in guidance are mangled and no longer need to be guided. The body you lovingly bathed is now bathed in its own blood. You gave your Son to the world, and this is how we return him to you.

Finally, the world understands who Jesus really is.

It's distressing to see you mourning like this, Mother. When you gave your fiat to the angel Gabriel, did you know how awful the end would be?

All: Mother, I want to somehow turn your mourning into joy. Let me inscribe your name into the hearts of others, so that one day all of humanity will become your children.

FOURTEENTH STATION

Jesus Is Laid in the Tomb

V: We adore you, O Christ, and we praise you.
R: Because by your holy Cross, you have redeemed the world.

Leader: The swaddling clothes you once wrapped him in have been transformed into a shroud. The warm cradle you once laid him in has been transformed into a cold, stone tomb. He sleeps, but not in the comfortable dreaming of an infant. How it must break your heart to say goodbye! Mothers are meant to nurture, not bury, their sons.

In spite of your sorrow, there's something in your sigh that seems reassuring. Is it knowing that Jesus promised to rise from the dead? Is it knowing that the victory over Satan has been won? Is it knowing that you now have many other sons and daughters who need you?

All: Mother, take me into your arms. I'm sorry for all the sins I've committed — all the sins I'll ever commit. You didn't have to accept me as your child, but you did because your love is limitless. Never let me stray from your love.

Concluding Prayer

Mother, thank you for the suffering you have endured for my sake, for the suffering you continue to endure whenever I fall victim to Satan's cunning. You know how deeply this hurts your Son, yet you forgive me every time, just as he does. Grant me the grace to embrace the cross as the two of you did, so that I may never be afraid to dare all for the Triune God.

Thank you for accepting me as your child and loving me unconditionally. I want to take you deeply into my heart and constantly give you all my love. Let me never forget that you are my hope, my joy, my mother. Lead me to your Son and help me to love him as much as you do. Amen.